No Backbone!
The World of Invertebrates
Squishy Sponges

by Natalie Lunis

Consultant: Bill Murphy
Marine Biologist, Northern Waters Gallery
New England Aquarium
Boston, MA

BEARPORT
PUBLISHING

NEW YORK, NEW YORK

Credits

Cover and TOC, © James D. Watt/SeaPics.com, © Styve Reineck/Shutterstock, © David Nielsam/Shutterstock and © Doug Perrine/SeaPics.com; Title Page, © David Nielsam/Shutterstock; 4–5, © Doug Perrine/SeaPics.com; 6T, © Jonathan Bird/SeaPics.com; 6M, © age fotostock/SuperStock; 6B, © Norbert Wu/Minden Pictures; 7, © Doug Perrine/SeaPics.com; 8, © age fotostock/SuperStock; 9, © Manuela Kirschner/Peter Arnold, Inc.; 11, © Doug Perrine/SeaPics.com; 12, © Franklin Viola/Animals Animals-Earth Scenes; 13, © Doug Perrine/SeaPics.com; 14T, © Franklin Viola/Animals Animals-Earth Scenes; 14B, © Marilyn & Maris Kazmers/SeaPics.com; 15, © Ross Armstrong/SeaPics.com; 16, © NHPA/Daniel Heuclin; 17, © Fred Bavendam/Minden Pictures; 18, © Corinne J. Humphrey/IndexStock; 19, © BIOS Klein & Hubert/Peter Arnold, Inc.; 20, © Victoria Short/Shutterstock; 21, © Doug Perrine/SeaPics.com; 22TL, © Chris Mc Laughlin/Animals Animals-Earth Scenes; 22TR, © Comstock Images/Alamy; 22BL, © Andrew J. Martinez/Photo Researchers, Inc.; 22BR, © Masa Ushioda/SeaPics.com; 22 Spot, © Styve Reineck/Shutterstock; 23TL, © Jim Wehtje/Photodisc Green/Getty Images; 23TR, © Nancy Louie/istockphoto.com; 23BL, © Doug Perrine/SeaPics.com; 23BR, © Tobias Bernhard/OSF/Animals Animals-Earth Scenes.

Publisher: Kenn Goin
Editorial Director: Adam Siegel
Creative Director: Spencer Brinker
Design: Dawn Beard Creative
Photo Researcher: Elaine Soares

Library of Congress Cataloging-in-Publication Data

Lunis, Natalie.
  Squishy sponges / by Natalie Lunis.
      p. cm. — (No backbone! The world of invertebrates)
  Includes bibliographical references and index.
  ISBN-13: 978-1-59716-512-9 (lib. bdg.)
  ISBN-10: 1-59716-512-3 (lib. bdg.)
  1. Sponges—Juvenile literature. I. Title.

  QL371.6.L86 2008
  593.4—dc22

                          2007016510

For more information, write to Bearport Publishing Company, Inc., 101 Fifth Avenue, Suite 6R, New York, New York 10003. Printed in the United States of America.

10 9 8 7 6 5 4 3 2 1

Contents

Underwater Animals

Sponges are animals that live in the sea.

They have no brains, hearts, or blood.

They have no heads, arms, or legs.

They don't move around.

For a long time, people thought they were underwater plants.

Sponges live in all the world's oceans.

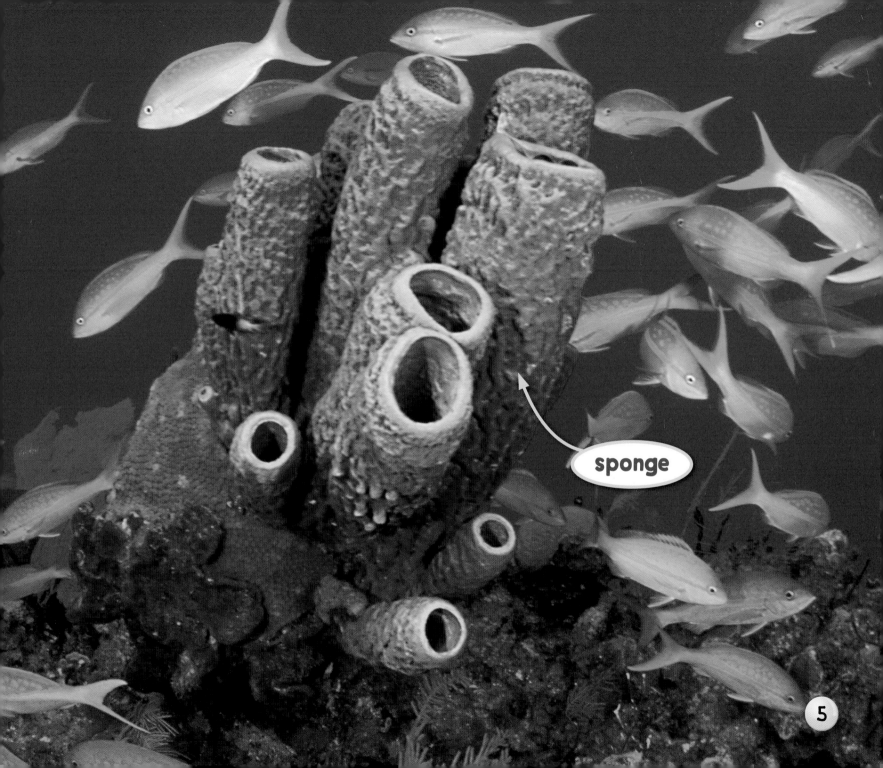

sponge

Staying in Shape

There are about 5,000 kinds of sponges.

The smallest are the size of a pea.

The tallest are taller than most people.

Sponges can be shaped like barrels, tubes, antlers, or rocks.

Sponges have no **backbones,** but many do have skeletons. Their skeletons help them keep their unusual shapes.

Staying in Place

Sponges spend almost all their lives in one place.

When a sponge is very young, it attaches itself to something hard.

Many attach themselves to rocks.

Others attach themselves to coral reefs.

Coral reefs are like underwater walls. They build up over many years from the skeletons of small animals called corals.

sponge

coral reef

Food That Flows In

Sponges cannot move around to get food.

Instead, water brings them all the food they need.

The water flows into openings called **pores** in a sponge's leathery skin.

Then it flows through tunnels and over the soft parts of the sponge's body.

The soft parts take tiny plants and animals from the water and feed on them.

The plants and animals that sponges eat are too tiny to see without a **microscope**.

Not Too Tasty

Sponges taste and smell bad.

Some even have poison in their bodies.

Most sea animals stay away from sponges, but a few are able to eat them.

A sponge's enemies include fish, **sea slugs**, snails, and turtles.

Most of the time, sponges don't die when parts of them are eaten. Instead, the bitten-off parts just grow back.

sea slug

A Popular Place

A sponge's body has many large and small openings.

These holes and tunnels are good hiding places for many animals.

Some fish, crabs, and shrimps even use sponges as homes.

Some of these animals go in and out of their underwater "apartments."

Others spend their whole lives inside a sponge.

One scientist counted more than 16,000 shrimps living inside one large sponge.

Carried Away

A few kinds of crabs use sponges in a surprising way.

They tear and snip off pieces of a sponge.

Then they carry the pieces on their backs.

This disguise helps the crabs hide from their enemies.

The pieces of sponge that a crab snips off continue to live and grow. After a while, they attach themselves to the crab's shell.

Household Helpers

More than 4,000 years ago, people started using sponges.

They brought the sponges up from the sea and left them out in the sun.

The skin and soft parts rotted away, and the squishy skeletons were left.

Greeks and Romans used them for washing and cleaning.

Soldiers used them to pad their helmets.

Only a few types of sponges have the kind of springy, squishy skeletons that people can use. Most kinds have hard, glass-like skeletons or hard, chalky skeletons.

19

From Sea to Factory

People still use sponges for washing and cleaning.

Most of the sponges people use today are not real sponge skeletons, however.

They are made in factories.

Yet they are like sea sponges in one important way.

They have many holes and tunnels that hold lots of water.

Today, scientists are working on another important use for sea sponges. They are trying to make new medicines from the animals' bodies.

21

A World of Invertebrates

Animals that have backbones are known as *vertebrates* (VUR-tuh-brits). Mammals, birds, fish, reptiles, and amphibians are all vertebrates.

Animals that don't have backbones are *invertebrates* (in-VUR-tuh-brits). Worms, jellyfish, crabs, and sponges are all invertebrates. So are all insects and spiders. More than 95 percent of all kinds of animals are invertebrates.

Sponges make up their own group of invertebrates. They have no close relatives in the animal world. Here are four different kinds of sponges.

Tube Sponge

Stove Pipe Sponge

Giant Barrel Sponge

Elephant Ear Sponge

Glossary

backbones
(BAK-*bohnz*)
a group of
connected bones
that run along
the backs of some
animals, such as
dogs, cats, and fish;
also called spines

microscope
(MYE-kruh-skope)
a tool that
scientists use to
see things that
are too small to
see with the
eyes alone

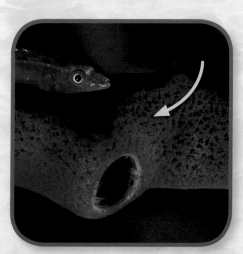

pores (PORZ)
small holes in a
sponge that let
water flow in

sea slugs
(SEE SLUHGZ)
snails without
shells that live in
the ocean and
are often brightly
colored

Index

Read More

Logue, Mary. *Sponges.* Chanhassen, MN: Child's World (2005).

Rake, Jody Sullivan. *Sponges.* Mankato, MN: Capstone Press (2007).

Stone, Lynn M. *Sponges: Science Under the Sea.* Vero Beach, FL: Rourke Publishing (2003).

Learn More Online

To learn more about sponges, visit **www.bearportpublishing.com/NoBackbone**